You
b

DO-IT-YOURSELF

WOODWORK IN THE HOME

WOODWORK IN THE HOME

A practical, illustrated guide to all the basic woodworking
tasks, in step-by-step pictures

Mike Collins

LORENZ BOOKS

This edition is published by Lorenz Books,
an imprint of Anness Publishing Ltd,
Blaby Road,
Wigston,
Leicestershire
LE18 4SE;
info@anness.com

www.lorenzbooks.com;
www.annesspublishing.com

If you like the images in this book and
would like to investigate using them for
publishing, promotions or advertising,
please visit our website
www.practicalpictures.com for more
information.

© Anness Publishing Limited 2013

Publisher: Joanna Lorenz
Art Manager: Clare Reynolds
Project Editor: Felicity Forster
Photographers: Colin Bowling & John Freeman
Illustrator: Peter Bull
Designer: Bill Mason
Production Controller: Wendy Lawson

Additional text: Diane Carr & Stephen Corbett

ACKNOWLEDGEMENTS AND NOTES
The publisher would like to thank The Tool Shop
for supplying tools for jacket photography:
97 Lower Marsh, Waterloo, London SE1 7AB
Tel 020 7207 2077; Fax 020 7207 5222
www.thetoolshop-diy.com

CONTENTS

INTRODUCTION

As a constructional material, wood is invaluable. It is very strong for its weight, and it can be used to create quite complex structures at relatively low cost. Properly looked after, wood will last for years, as an examination of your surroundings will confirm. All homes, no matter how they have been built, will contain a large amount of wood. The basic framework of the house may be made of wood, as well as at least some internal walls and the structure supporting the roof. Floors often have wooden surfaces – the material is warmer underfoot than concrete and stone; walls will be trimmed at floor level and around door openings with wooden mouldings, while the doors themselves will almost certainly be wood; window frames, too, are commonly of wooden construction. Then there is the furniture – shelves, cabinets, chairs, tables and so on. So sooner or later the do-it-yourselfer will be faced with tackling some form of woodworking task.

Fortunately, wood is an easy and forgiving material to work with, requiring few specialized tools unless undertaking cabinet-making or similar complex jobs. Taking the time to develop a few basic, practical

LEFT: Wood possesses a wide range of characteristics in varying degrees – strength, durability, flexibility, brittleness and, of course, beauty. Woodwork is involved in all sorts of jobs around the home, such as putting up shelves, fitting architraves (trims), replacing doors and drawers, and fitting locks.

ABOVE: Skirtings (baseboards) protect wall surfaces at floor level from accidental damage. They receive a lot of wear and tear from feet, vacuum cleaners and furniture legs, and may need replacing.

ABOVE: Renewing old drawer fronts is neither a complex nor a very expensive job. Remove the old drawer front from the carcass with a screwdriver, drill pilot holes in the new front, and screw it into position.

woodworking skills will allow you to tackle a wide variety of do-it-yourself tasks – from simply giving a wooden surface (such as a floor) a new finish, through putting up the simplest of fixtures, to carrying out all manner of repairs around the home.

The following pages contain a selection of simple indoor projects that involve working with wood. By using the information provided, you will gain the confidence you need to

complete many do-it-yourself tasks. Just remember that, as with so many things, care and patience are the most important keys to success.

RIGHT: Shelving systems such as these adjustable brackets are capable of holding heavy weights, and have the advantage of being portable when you need to move them. The bracket positions can be adjusted to vary the spacing between the shelves, but remember that a shelf's capacity depends on the strength of the wall fixings employed.

MATERIALS & EQUIPMENT

Wood can be purchased in two basic forms: as sections of natural timber (lumber) sawn and/or planed to shape, or as manufactured boards made from thin veneers, wood particles or blocks. All have their specific uses, and it is important to choose the right type for the job in hand. Despite the introduction of power tools in recent years, few jobs can be done without using hand tools at some stage of the process, and every do-it-yourselfer will gradually collect more of them as the need arises. There is a wide variety of tools to choose from, as browsing through any catalogue will reveal, and the following pages include most of the materials and tools in common use, as well as a guide to safety equipment.

WOOD AND MANUFACTURED BOARDS

As they are expensive, hardwoods are often used as veneers over cheaper materials, as lippings around flat surfaces such as shelving and table tops, and for picture framing.

Softwoods, such as pine and, to a lesser extent, Douglas fir, are the most commonly used types of wood for do-it-yourself jobs, such as wall frames, flooring, skirtings (baseboards), picture and dado (chair) rails, and a great variety of cladding, framing and fencing applications. In addition to softwoods, there is a range of inexpensive manufactured boards.

PRACTICAL USES

The two boards most often used are plywood and chipboard (particle board). The former, which has good mechanical strength and can be sawn easily, is suitable for structural work.

Chipboard is more friable and less easy to work accurately, but is cheap. It is adequate for some flooring applications and a host of carcassing jobs, such as kitchen cabinets and bookcases. It is unwise to drive screws or nails into the edge of a chipboard panel, as the material will crumble.

Both plywood and chipboard are available faced with hardwood and coloured melamine veneer for improved appearance.

Blockboard, which consists of solid wooden blocks sandwiched between plywood skins, is a stable and strong

ABOVE: Beech hardwood.

structural material often used where some form of weight-bearing capacity is required. As with all manufactured boards, the extremely hard resins used to bond blockboard together rapidly blunt tools unless they are tungsten (carbide) tipped.

Pineboard is like the core of blockboard, but without the outer layers. Small strips of pine are glued together on edge and sanded smooth. It is ideal for shelving and carcassing.

MDF (medium-density fiberboard) is another useful material. Unlike most other boards, it can be worked to fine detail with saws and chisels, and it is often used for delicate mouldings.

Hardboard is ideal for covering floors prior to tiling or carpeting and, as it is light, for making back panels for cabinets and pictures. It can be used for making templates to establish correct shapes, helping to avoid mistakes when using expensive material for a finished piece.

ABOVE: Pine softwood.

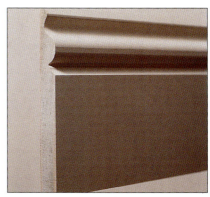

ABOVE: Paper-coated MDF skirting (baseboard).

STANDARD SIZES

Nearly all manufactured boards have a standard size of 1220 x 2440mm (4 x 8ft). Some suppliers offer a metric size, which is smaller (1200 x 2400mm), so always check, as this can make a critical difference to your cutting list. Special sizes of plywood and MDF, up to 3m (10ft) in length, are available from some suppliers. Many stores will offer part sheets or cut large sheets into smaller sizes if requested at the time of purchase.

GRAIN DIRECTION

The direction in which the grain runs on the outer layers is always given first when describing plywood. This can be important when planning your cutting list. With birch plywood, for example, 1220 x 2440mm (4 x 8ft) in a supplier's catalogue will indicate that the grain runs across the width of the board, not down its length. Most veneered decorative boards have the grain running across the length, so their catalogue entry would read 2440 x 1220mm (8 x 4ft).

COMMON THICKNESSES OF MANUFACTURED BOARDS

TYPE	3mm ⅛in	6mm ¼in	9mm ⅜in	12mm ½in	16mm ⅝in	19mm ¾in	22mm ⅞in	25mm 1in	32mm 1¼in
Plywood	✓	✓	✓	✓	✓	✓	✓	✓	
Plywood (D. fir)			✓		✓				
Blockboard						✓		✓	
Chipboard				✓	✓	✓	✓	✓	
Hardboard	✓	✓							
MDF		✓	✓	✓		✓		✓	✓

JOINT PLATES AND HINGES

There is a huge range of fittings available for making joints and connecting different materials. These will often prevent the need for making complex joints in wood, allowing the less skilled to produce strong structures or repairs with relative ease.

Hinges will be found all around the home on doors and cabinets, and replacing or refitting them is a common do-it-yourself task.

JOINT PLATES AND BRACKETS

Flat mild-steel plates, drilled and countersunk to take wood screws, are a common means of making and strengthening butt joints in wooden framing. Some commonly used joint plates are L-shaped corner plates and T-shaped fixing plates.

Brackets such as corner plate fixings, 90-degree angle brackets and joist hangers are also available. They can be used to make right-angled joints, overlapping joints and for hanging joists.

HINGES

Any device that includes a pivot action can be called a hinge, and there are many different variations. Some are designed to be concealed within the framework of a cabinet, or the carcass, while others are intended to act as decorative features in their own right.

It is important to fit the correct number of hinges of a suitable size and robustness when hanging a door so that it is well supported when it swings open. If a hinge or hinge pin is strained

ABOVE: An L-shaped corner plate.

ABOVE: A simple 90-degree angle bracket.

in any way, the door will not fit in the frame properly and may even become detached, possibly causing injury.

ABOVE: Hinges are available in a wide range of types, finishes, sizes and materials for a variety of tasks. Some are functional, while others make decorative features in their own right.

ABOVE: A T-shaped fixing plate.

ABOVE: A corner plate fixing.

ABOVE: An overlapping fixing plate.

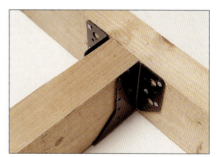

ABOVE: A joist hanger.

KNOCK-DOWN JOINTS

These fittings are often used with manufactured boards, such as chipboard (particle board) and plywood. They ensure good, square connections, usually by means of pegs, and allow the assembly to be dismantled and reassembled as required. For the best results, at least two joints should be fitted between each pair of panels.

ABOVE: The knock-down joint in its separate parts ready for assembly.

ABOVE: When the parts are connected, they form a strong and accurate joint.

BASIC TOOLS

The tools featured here will allow you to tackle a variety of do-it-yourself jobs where wood is involved. If your budget is tight, buy several hand tools rather than one power tool.

A measuring tape is needed to ensure accurate measurements.

A spirit (carpenter's) level is essential for finding a true horizontal or vertical.

A flat rule is needed for marking out. You can choose from wood, steel or plastic. When measuring curves, however, a flexible steel rule or a retractable steel tape will provide greater accuracy.

A T-square is useful for marking out large sheets of board, but it must be used on a straight edge to give a 90-degree line across the sheet.

Use a mortise gauge to scribe two parallel lines directly on to wood. Its steel pins are adjustable, while the sliding stock runs against the face of the work. Some have a single fixed pin on the opposite side for gauging thickness.

A craft knife that stores extra blades in the handle is ideal for many tasks.

The most common saw for home use is the cross-cut hand saw, which is used for large sections of wood. A tenon saw is used for smaller work and a mitre box will allow you to make 45-degree cuts.

For drilling holes, a cordless drill will be most convenient.

For smoothing and trimming wood, you will need a plane, the best choice being a small jack, or smoothing, plane.

A small selection of chisels will cover most needs, and those with bevelled

measuring tape

spirit (carpenter's) level

mortise gauge

cordless drill

edges are the most versatile. Keep them sharp and guarded when not in use. Only drive them with a wooden mallet, and keep your hands behind the cutting edge at all times.

You will require a few screwdrivers of different sizes, with blades for slotted, Phillips and Pozidriv screws. Always use the correct size for the screw, or you may damage the head.

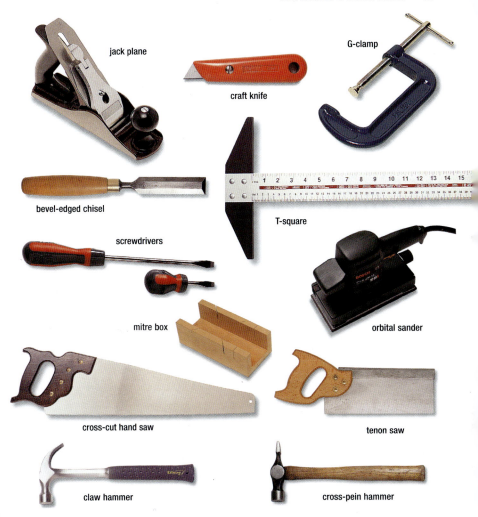

jack plane

craft knife

G-clamp

bevel-edged chisel

screwdrivers

T-square

mitre box

orbital sander

cross-cut hand saw

tenon saw

claw hammer

cross-pein hammer

The most essential hammer for the do-it-yourselfer is the claw hammer, with a weight of about 365–450g (13–16oz). This will be heavy enough to drive quite large nails. For lighter nails, choose a cross-pein hammer, using its flat head to start small fixings between your fingers. For small panel pins (brads), a pin hammer will be very useful.

Various forms of clamp are available for holding sections of a piece of work together while a permanent fixing is made. The G-clamp is a general-purpose tool; invest in a few different sizes.

Sanding and shaping are important do-it-yourself techniques, and they are much easier with a power sander. For general use, an orbital sander is by far the most versatile power tool to buy.

NAILS, SCREWS AND DRILL BITS

There is no such thing as an "ordinary" nail. All nails have been designed for specific purposes, although some can be put to several uses.

Wire, lost-head and oval nails can be used for general carpentry. Oval nails can be driven below the surface of the work with less likelihood of them splitting the wood.

Cut nails have a tapering, rectangular section, which gives them excellent holding properties. They are largely used for fixing flooring.

Panel pins (brads) are used for fixing thin panels and cladding. They are nearly always punched below the surface, as are veneer pins.

When there is a need to secure thin or fragile sheet material, such as plasterboard (gypsum board), large-headed nails are used. These are commonly called clout nails, but may also be found under specific names, such as plasterboard nails.

The holding power of screws is much greater than that of nails, and items that have been screwed together can easily be taken apart again without damage to the components.

There are various types of screw head, the most common being the slotted screw head, followed by the Phillips head and the Pozidriv head, both of which have a cruciform pattern to take the screwdriver blade.

Drill bits come in a bewildering array of sizes and types but only a few are needed by the do-it-yourselfer, such as dowel bits for flat-bottomed holes, flat bits, which cut large holes very rapidly, and twist bits, which make small holes and are used for starting screws.

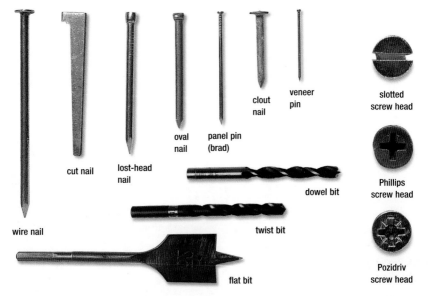

clout nail

veneer pin

slotted screw head

oval nail

panel pin (brad)

cut nail

lost-head nail

dowel bit

Phillips screw head

wire nail

twist bit

flat bit

Pozidriv screw head

FIXTURES

Installing new fixtures is a basic do-it-yourself activity that covers a variety of tasks, such as hanging a picture, fitting drawer and door handles, putting up lightweight shelving, and fitting hooks, locks, clasps and catches on all manner of items. Many are very straightforward jobs, which involve simply screwing, pinning or sticking the fixture in place.

WALL PLUGS AND BOLTS

Plastic wall plugs are the most common method of providing fixings in solid walls. They expand to grip the sides of the hole when a wooden screw is driven home. They must be a snug fit in their holes, otherwise they will not hold.

A wall bolt also expands within its hole, and is often used when a heavy load is expected, such as when fitting heavy timbers to brickwork. A washer should be used under the nut to prevent damage to the wood.

HOOKS

Fixtures of this kind include coat hooks, cup hooks and dozens of other quickly fitted aids and clips of all types. Threaded hooks and eyes need a pilot hole to be made with a bradawl, after which they can be screwed in place with finger and thumb.

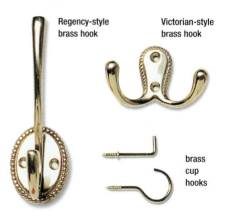

Regency-style brass hook

Victorian-style brass hook

brass cup hooks

SHELF SUPPORTS

Small shelves can be supported in a variety of ways, including using plastic fittings, screw eyes, dowels and lengths of wood. All these methods are suitable for shelving that will carry little weight.

ABOVE: A selection of wall plugs and screws in different sizes.

ABOVE: A variety of very lightweight plastic shelf fittings.

SAFETY EQUIPMENT

Your personal safety should underlie every stage of woodworking practice, including the layout of a workshop. It is better to plan your work to eliminate hazards rather than accommodate them – for example, using a dust extractor on a machine that creates a lot of dust is a better solution than wearing a dust mask. Because working with wood depends on the use of cutting tools, this may seem a risk that cannot be avoided, but any professional will tell you that a sharp tool is actually less dangerous than a blunt one or a tool that is used incorrectly.

SAFETY EQUIPMENT

Even though a private workshop is not required to comply with the health and safety legislation that applies to commercial premises, it makes sense to observe the same safety disciplines and use the personal protection equipment that is recommended and readily available. One particular danger to be aware of is fire, since wood is inflammable and so are some of the materials used when working with wood. It is advisable not to smoke when working with materials that are flammable, and make sure you always have a fire extinguisher to hand.

fire extinguisher

FIRST AID KIT

Obtain the correct size of kit recommended for small workshops, and keep it in a prominent position ready for use. If any of the contents are used, replace them immediately.

first aid kit

EYE PROTECTION

Always protect your eyes with safety glasses or goggles when sanding, finishing or using power tools. When operating a machine that produces large quantities of chippings at high speed, wear a full-face visor.

safety goggles

EAR PROTECTION

When using power tools or machinery, wear approved ear protectors or earplugs to keep noise to an acceptable level. Some people think that it is safer to operate a machine by listening to its performance. They are wrong, and they risk permanent impairment of their hearing in the future.

ear protectors

DUST EXTRACTION

By far the best way of reducing the risk of inhaling sawdust is to install a dust extraction system. Compact units designed for the small workshop are available from all good tool suppliers. Many portable power tools have self-contained dust extraction systems or are supplied with adaptors for direct connection to an extraction unit.

DUST MASKS

There are several types of mask to choose from, including the frame mask with replaceable pads and disposable masks that cover the whole of the mouth and nose. Choose the right product for the level of dust

dust mask

generated in the workshop. The dust produced by sanding machines is the most hazardous and needs a mask with a fine filter. Use sanders that are fitted with their own dust collection bag to cut down on the amount of dust produced. Clear, full-face safety masks are available and are easy to put on and comfortable to wear, especially when using power tools.

When working with hazardous finishing materials, keep the workshop well ventilated and wear a respirator if necessary. Always be guided by the manufacturer's safety data, which by law must be supplied with any hazardous product. In general, if a product is so dangerous as to cause potentially serious problems, you should consider an alternative.

GLOVES AND BOOTS

It is advisable to wear heavy-duty rigger's gloves when handling sawn wood or large, heavy sheets of material. When you are using adhesives or finishing materials that are harmful to the skin, wear rubber or latex gloves. It is best to wear sensible and sturdy boots to keep toes protected

gloves

in case you drop any wood or a sharp or heavy tool.

PERSONAL SAFETY

- Avoid wearing loose clothing and jewellery when working, especially with machinery and power tools.
- Stout boots should be worn – a sheet of plywood will be painful if it slips and lands on your toe. You can prevent this by wearing leather gloves when handling wood.
- Always inspect wood for splinters and protruding nails before picking it up.
- Always have a first aid kit in the workshop for minor injuries.
- When you work on large machines, do not work alone in case of injury.

SHELVES & WALLS

You can never have too much storage space, and shelves are an important means of providing it. You can make shelves yourself or you can install a versatile, adjustable ready-made shelving system. Both are easy to fit. All walls incorporate wooden fixtures of one form or another. At the very least, there will be skirtings (baseboards) at floor level and wooden trims around door openings. In some cases, there may be dado (chair) rails and, in older properties, picture rails near the ceiling. At some stage, you may find that you need to replace these items, either to effect repairs or give the room a new look. Cladding the walls with wooden boards or panels is another means of giving a room a fresh look, and can provide thermal and acoustic insulation too.

FITTING SHELVES

Putting up shelves is a fundamental do-it-yourself task, and is probably one of the first jobs the newcomer will tackle. With a little thought, shelving can be made to be decorative as well as functional, and wood can be used to good effect.

The essential requirements of fitting shelving are establishing a truly level surface with a spirit (carpenter's) level, obtaining firm fixings in the wall and being able to fit accurately into an alcove.

PLANNING SHELVES

Consider how to make best use of the new storage space. Make a rough sketch of the layout, taking into account aspects of the items that will be stored, such as the height and width of books, or the clearance that ornaments and photographs require. Aim to keep everyday items within easy reach, which in practice is between about 750mm (2ft 6in) and 1.5m (5ft) above the floor. Position deep shelves near the bottom so that it is easy to see and reach to the back. Allow 25–50mm (1–2in) of clearance above the height of the objects to be stored, so that they are easy to take down and put back.

Think about weight too. If the shelves will support heavy objects, the shelving material must be chosen with care, since thin shelves will sag if heavily loaded, unless they are well supported. With 12mm (½in) chipboard (particle board) and ready-made veneered or melamine-faced shelves, space brackets at 450mm (18in) intervals for heavy loads or up to 600mm (2ft) for light loads. With 19mm (¾in) chipboard or 12mm (½in) plywood, increase the spacing to 600mm (2ft) and 750mm (2ft 6in) respectively. For 19mm (¾in) plywood, blockboard, MDF (medium-density fiberboard) or natural wood, the bracket spacing can be 750mm (2ft 6in) for heavy loads and 900mm (3ft) for light ones.

FITTING BRACKETS AND SHELVES

Use your spirit level to ascertain the height and horizontal run of the shelf, then mark the positions for the brackets. Mark the positions of the screws through the holes in the brackets, drill with a masonry bit and insert wall plugs. Hold each bracket in place and start all the screws into the wall plugs before tightening them fully. This will ensure that they engage properly.

If fitting more than one shelf on an uninterrupted run of wall, mark them out at the same time, using a try or combination square. Cut them to size, then screw them to the shelf brackets.

You can also attach the shelf to the brackets before mounting the brackets to the wall.

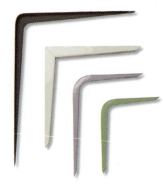

FITTING SHELF BRACKETS

1 Mark the position of the shelf by drawing a line across the wall, using a long, straight batten as a guide. Make sure it is perfectly horizontal with a spirit (carpenter's) level.

2 Mark the positions of the fixing screws on the wall through the bracket holes. For accuracy, lay a short piece of wood on top of each bracket, aligning it with the pencil line.

3 Drill the holes for the screws, using a masonry bit if necessary, and insert wall plugs. Hold each bracket in place and start all of its screws before tightening them fully.

4 Lay the shelf on top of the brackets, making sure the overhang is equal at each end. Use a bradawl to make pilot holes and screw through the brackets into the shelf.

FITTING SHELVING SYSTEMS

Shelving systems abound in do-it-yourself stores for those who prefer simply to fit rather than to make the shelving. There is a range of brackets on the market to cater for every need, and these clip into slotted uprights screwed to the wall. The bracket positions can be adjusted to vary the spacing between the shelves to accommodate your needs.

Shelving systems are a versatile way of dealing with changing requirements, and they have the distinct advantage of being portable when you need to move them. They are capable of holding heavy weights, but remember that ultimately a shelf's capacity depends on the strength of the wall fixings used.

INSTALLING THE SHELVING

First, measure the distance between the shelving uprights, bearing in mind the thickness and construction of the shelving material. Books can be very heavy, so do not set the uprights too far apart, otherwise the shelf will sag in the middle. About a quarter of the length of the shelf can overhang each end. If necessary, cut the uprights to length. Drill and plug the wall so that you can attach one upright by its topmost hole. Do not tighten the screw fully at this stage.

Hold your spirit (carpenter's) level against the side of the upright, and when you are satisfied that it is vertical, mark its position lightly on the wall with a pencil line. Mark in the remaining screw positions, then drill and plug the rest of the screw holes. Install subsequent uprights by using the first as a guide.

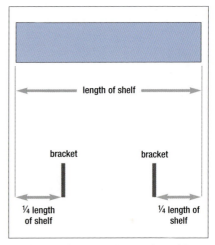

1 Calculate the distance between the uprights and mark their positions on the wall. Do not set the uprights too far apart, otherwise the shelf may sag between them.

4 If the wall is uneven, use scraps of card as packing material where necessary. Alternatively, accommodate any discrepancies by varying the tightness of the screws.

2 Drill and plug the wall for the top screw of the first upright. Hold the upright in place and insert the screw, but do not tighten it fully, allowing the upright to hang freely.

3 Check that the bracket is absolutely vertical with a spirit (carpenter's) level. Then mark the remaining screw positions on the wall. Drill and plug them, and fit the screws.

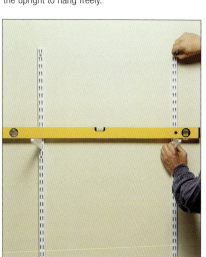

5 To mark the position of the second upright, use the first as a guide. Simply fit a shelf bracket into each upright and level them with the aid of a spirit level. Fit the second upright.

6 The slots in the uprights allow the shelf brackets to be inserted at varying heights and it is very easy to reposition the brackets whenever necessary.

FITTING SHELVES IN AN ALCOVE

An easy way to measure the internal width of an alcove is by using two overlapping wooden battens. Allow them to touch each end of the alcove and clamp them together on the overlap. Transfer this measurement to the shelving material and carefully cut it to length.

If the sides of the alcove appear uneven, take measurements across the back of the alcove and the front. Use the shorter of the two dimensions and disguise any gaps with quadrant moulding (base shoe).

The simplest method of supporting a shelf in an alcove is to fit horizontal battens to the back and side walls. For a neat appearance, make the side battens about 25mm (1in) shorter than the depth of the shelf and cut the facing ends at an angle. This will make them less obvious.

Establish the position for the back batten with a spirit (carpenter's) level. Drill and plug the holes, then screw the batten into place. Using the back batten as a reference point, fit the side battens to the end walls of the alcove.

Drill screw clearance holes in the shelf, place the shelf on the battens and screw it down. When fitting more than one shelf into an alcove, do not cut all the shelves to the same size. If the sides of the alcove are plasterwork, brick or stone, there will almost certainly be some discrepancies in

1 Use two battens clamped together to measure the width of an alcove. Where the wall is masonry or plastered, measure the back and front of the alcove, as they may differ.

the width between the top and bottom, so measure for each shelf individually and cut them separately.

If there is an uneven gap along the back of a shelf, caused by an uneven wall surface, you can hide the gap by pinning quadrant moulding along the back edge of the shelf.

TIP

If you want to fit a shelf accurately to an uneven wall, hold a piece of cardboard on top of the support battens and run a pencil and block of wood along the wall to transfer the shape to the card. Then cut the card to shape and use it as a template for the shelf.

2 Lay the battens on top of the shelf material and transfer the measurement to the wood. Cut the shelf to length. Repeat the process for any other shelves.

3 Cut a batten to fit the alcove and support the back edge of the shelf. Mark its position with the aid of a spirit (carpenter's) level, drill and plug holes in the wall and screw it into place.

4 Cut short battens to support each end of the shelf, mark their positions, using the back batten as a guide. Then screw them into place on the end walls of the alcove.

5 Check that the shelf fits properly. Then drill countersunk screw clearance holes in either end and along the back edge. Screw the shelf to the support battens from the top.

USING MOULDINGS

Moulding is the term used to describe any section of wood that has been shaped, either by hand or by machinery, to alter the square profile of the original piece. This may range from simply rounding over the sharp edges of the finished work to adding more decorative detail.

TYPICAL APPLICATIONS

Mouldings have many uses, not only providing protection to vulnerable surfaces, but also adding decoration. The larger mouldings include architraves (trims), dado (chair) rails, picture rails and skirtings (baseboards). Architraves are fitted around flush door and window openings to create decorative and protective borders. Dado and picture rails are horizontal mouldings fixed to wall surfaces, the former to protect the plaster from damage by the backs of chairs, and the latter to allow pictures to be hung. Skirtings are boards fixed at ground level to protect the plaster from damage by feet or furniture.

FIXING MOULDINGS

Generally speaking, it is wise to drill pilot holes in hardwood mouldings before nailing, especially when fixing close to the ends, since small-section hardwoods, especially ramin, which is often used, will split readily.

Softwoods are far more forgiving, and it is unnecessary to drill a softwood architrave before nailing it in place. Simply drive the nails in, punch the heads below the surface, and fill before finishing. Panel pins (brads) or lost-head oval wire nails are the preferred fixings for architraves.

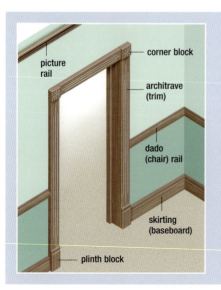

picture rail

corner block

architrave (trim)

dado (chair) rail

skirting (baseboard)

plinth block

PRACTICALITIES

This is a typical layout showing how architectural mouldings are put to use. They are so called because they would be used to produce a certain effect in the interior of a room rather than for individual items of furniture.

Notice how they combine a decorative effect with good practical points: the plinth blocks and corner blocks around a door frame convey a classic formality, but they also avoid the need to form complex joints where two wooden components meet.

The plinth blocks provide useful protection to more intricate mouldings at floor level where they may be damaged easily.

FITTING A SHELF MOULDING

1 Using a try or combination square, check that the corners of the board are square. If necessary, plane or re-cut the edges to ensure that they are square.

2 Mark the mouldings to length and, using a tenon saw and mitre box, cut their ends at 45 degrees to fit neatly together at the corners of the board.

3 Check the fit of the mouldings, then apply glue to them and the edges of the board. Hold them in place with plenty of masking tape and leave for the glue to dry.

4 When the glue has dried, clamp the board securely to your bench top and carefully clean up any rough edges or slight overlaps with a plane. Finish by sanding lightly.

FITTING AN ARCHITRAVE

Trimming a door is fairly straightforward. Measure the internal width of the door frame and mark out the top piece of architrave (trim) so that its bottom edge is 12mm (½in) longer. Mitre the ends at 45 degrees, using a mitre box, so that the top edge is longer than the bottom.

Pin the top piece of architrave to the top of the frame so that it projects by an equal amount at each side and is 6mm (¼in) up from the bottom edge of the top frame member. All architrave should be set about 6mm (¼in) back from the inside edge of the door frame.

Measure for each side piece separately, as they can vary quite considerably over the width of a door, especially in older houses. Cut each to length, mitring the top ends to match the horizontal section already fitted. Sand the ends to remove any splinters, then offer them up, checking the fit of the mitred ends. If all is well, pin the mouldings to the frame.

Drive all the pin heads below the surface of the wood with a nail punch. Then fill the holes and any gaps between the mitred ends of the architrave, using a coloured wood filler if you intend applying a translucent finish. Finally, when the filler is dry, sand it flush with the surrounding surface.

1 Remove the old architrave (trim) with a crowbar (wrecking bar). Place a block of wood beneath the tool's blade to protect the adjacent wall from damage.

4 Pin the new piece of architrave in place, making sure that it is horizontal and about 6mm (¼in) above the bottom face of the top internal frame member.

2 Pull out any remaining nails and scrape away any old wood filler or paint from the face of the opening's frame. Take care, however, not to gouge the wood.

3 Measure the internal width of the door frame and cut the top section of architrave to length, allowing for the 6mm (¼in) projection at each end. Mitre the ends at 45 degrees.

5 Measure, cut and fit the side pieces of architrave in the same manner. Pin them in position, butting their mitred ends against the ends of the top piece.

6 Punch all the pin heads below the surface of the wood, apply filler and sand it down. Any gaps between the mitred ends should also be filled and sanded smooth.

REPLACING SKIRTING BOARDS

Skirtings (baseboards) receive a lot of wear and tear from scuffing by feet and furniture, which is why they are there in the first place, of course. From time to time, after replacing floorboards or laying new woodstrip or laminate flooring, for example, the damage may be so great that sections of skirting or even complete lengths of it need to be replaced.

Skirtings may vary from simple rectangular sections of wood to quite ornate moulded profiles.

FITTING NEW SKIRTING BOARDS

In a rectangular room, it is always best to fit the two long sections of skirting board first, then fit the shorter ones to them. It makes handling, lifting and fixing much easier.

REPLACING STRAIGHT SECTIONS

To replace sections of skirting, first prise the old board partially away from the wall, using a crowbar (wrecking bar), then insert wedges to hold it far enough away to allow you to get at it with a saw. Place a mitre box tight against the board and, with a tenon saw, nibble away at it at 45 degrees until the board is cut in half. Repeat the 45-degree cut at the other end of the section to be replaced and remove the length of old skirting. Then offer up the replacement section, mark each

end with a pencil and mitre accordingly. Mitring the ends will make the joints between the new and old boards less obvious and easier to fill if there is any subsequent shrinkage.

A good way to hold the new section in position is to lay a plank so that it butts up against the skirting and kneel on it while driving the nails home. Set all nail heads below the surface before filling and sanding.

DEALING WITH CORNERS

When fitting a moulded shape into a corner, the best way to achieve the joint is to scribe it. This is done by marking the profile of one board on to the back of the other with the aid of a small offcut of the moulding. Then a coping saw is used to cut along the marked line, allowing the board to fit neatly over its neighbour. This technique avoids the mismatch of ends that can occur when some mouldings are mitred at 45 degrees, using a mitre box or mitre saw. However, to form an external corner for a wall return, use a mitre saw or mitre box in the normal way.

TIP

Many skirtings (baseboards) are fixed with flooring, or cut, nails, which are square-edged and grip extremely well. However, they may split a small section of replacement skirting, so use masonry nails instead and drill pilot holes through the skirting.

REPLACING A SECTION OF SKIRTING (BASEBOARD)

1 Prise away the old skirting (baseboard) with a crowbar (wrecking bar) and wedges.

2 Cut away the damaged section with a mitre box and a saw.

3 Hold a new length of board in place and mark it for cutting.

4 Hammer nails into the new section of board while holding a plank against the wood.

INTERNAL AND EXTERNAL MITRES OF A SKIRTING BOARD

ABOVE: An internal corner with mitred joint.

ABOVE: A mitred external corner.

REPLACING RAILS

Picture rails and dado rails, sometimes called chair rails because they protect the walls from damage by chair backs, may need to be renewed or repaired. This task is essentially the same as replacing skirtings (baseboards).

REMOVING AND REPLACING RAILS

Use a crowbar (wrecking bar) to prise the old picture or dado (chair) rail away from the wall, inserting a block of wood under its head to protect the plaster and to give extra leverage.

Remove any nails that remain in the wall with a pair of pincers, again using a block of wood to protect the wall. Make good the nail holes with filler, leaving it slightly proud at this stage. When the filler is completely dry, sand it down with abrasive paper wrapped around a cork block, or block of wood, to give a perfectly flat, smooth surface. Fit the new length of rail, scribing or mitring the ends as necessary to ensure a neat finish at the corners.

FIXING METHODS

Cut-nails, such as those used to fix skirtings, have long been used to fix picture rails, dado rails and the like, but you may find that they are not available in your local store. Any ordinary wire lost-head nail is a good alternative when fixing through plasterwork into stud (dry) walling, as long as you know where the studs are. With a brick or blockwork wall, use masonry nails, drilling clearance holes in the wood to prevent splits.

REPLACING A DADO RAIL

1 Prise the old rail from the wall using a crowbar (wrecking bar) and levering against a block of wood. This will provide additional leverage and prevent damage to the wall.

CUTTING A SCRIBED JOINT

Use a scrap of the moulding as a guide. Hold a pencil against the scrap of wood and run it over the back of the board to transfer the outline. Cut out the waste with a coping saw.

2 Remove any nails that remain in the wall with pincers. Again, lever against a block of wood to prevent the plasterwork from becoming damaged, reducing the amount of making good required.

3 Brush off all dust and loose paint and plaster. Fill any cracks or holes in the plasterwork with filler, working it in well with a filling or putty knife and leaving it slightly proud.

4 Leave the filler to dry. Then sand it with abrasive paper wrapped around a cork or wooden sanding block to obtain a smooth, flat finish. You may need to fill any low spots again.

5 Nail the new rail to the wall, making sure that it is horizontal with a spirit (carpenter's) level. Punch the nail heads below the surface of the wood, fill and sand smooth.

FIXING CLADDING

Wooden cladding may be fixed to walls and ceilings for a variety of reasons. These include: cosmetic, to hide the existing finish; acoustic, to deaden sound; and thermal, to insulate against heat loss. Sometimes cladding has a structural purpose, for example, when it forms part of a stud (dry) wall.

The framework of battens needs to be designed around obstacles (windows and doorways), electrical switches and sockets, and positioned so that whole sheets of cladding join on a stud.

BATTENING A WALL

Drill pilot holes in the battens for the masonry nails, as this will prevent the wood from splitting. Hammer a masonry nail home at one end, level the batten with a spirit (carpenter's) level and drive home a nail at the other end. Finish by driving in more nails along the batten. If the wall is crumbly, you can attach the battens with screws and wall plugs. Secure battening is essential.

FITTING SHEET PANELLING

Cladding can be fixed to the framework of battens using either nails or screws. If screws are used, especially brass ones, a feature can be made of them, so they should be equally spaced to form a pattern. Alternatively, a panel adhesive can be used. If it fails to adhere immediately, tap nails part way through into the battens. The nails can be removed when the panels are secure.

To cut cladding, use either a hand saw or power saw. If using a hand saw,

ABOVE: Cladding comes in a range of profiles and can be fixed to a framework of battens using nails, screws or adhesive.

ABOVE: Make sure joints coincide with the centres of studs.

have the decorative face uppermost and cut on the downstroke to limit the chances of damaging it. With a power saw, turn the decorative face of the wood downward. Before using the saw, score the cutting line carefully using a straightedge as a guide. If you need a perfectly straight edge on a cut sheet, where it is to be butted against another board, clamp a straightedge to the board as a guide for the saw.

After cutting, use a fine abrasive paper wrapped around a wood or cork block to smooth down the rough edges.

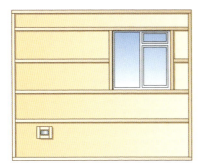 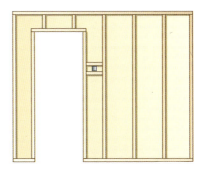

ABOVE: The framework of battens has to be tailored to suit the size and position of obstacles such as doors, windows and electrical fittings. Shown are layouts for vertical cladding (left) with a likely cable point and horizontal cladding (right).

LEFT: Work from each end of the surface to be covered, using cut panels in the middle to retain symmetry.

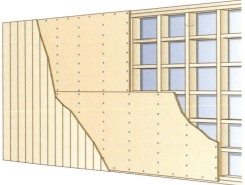

LEFT: Vertical boards fitted to stud (dry) walling with optional intermediate backing sheets. Note how the sheets meet in the centres of the studs.

TONGUED-AND-GROOVED BOARDING

Fitting tongued-and-grooved boarding is more time-consuming than using sheet materials, but the supporting framework can be made simpler because the boards are relatively narrow and rigid. As with all cladding, it is essential to ensure that the battens are fixed securely, and are reasonably spaced for adequate support.

FITTING THE BOARDING

First, square off the ends of the board to ensure that it is at 90 degrees, or 45 degrees if you want to set the boards at an angle. Mark off the length of board required with a craft knife or pencil and cut it to size with a tenon saw.

Place the board in position on the battens, making sure that the tongue is left exposed for the next board to slot over, and in the case of TGV (tongued, grooved and V-jointed) that the correct face side with the chamfer is showing.

Secret nail the board by driving panel pins (brads) through the tongue. Repeat this procedure with the remaining boards, tapping each firmly home with a mallet and an offcut of wood to prevent damage to the tongue before nailing.

Leave the second to last board slipped over the previous tongue, but before nailing, use an offcut and pencil to scribe the cutting line on the final board if it needs trimming to fit. Cut and plane the board to width. You might need to fit the last two boards by springing them into place, in which case, both will have to be nailed through the face, since the tongues will not be accessible. Punch the nail heads down and fill.

At internal and external corners, the joints between boards can be concealed by pinning on a decorative moulding, which can also be used along the ceiling. Fit normal skirtings (baseboards) at floor level.

DEALING WITH CORNERS

ABOVE: Neaten internal corners by pinning or gluing a length of scotia (cove) moulding into the angle. Use this at ceiling level too.

ABOVE: Butt-join the two boards that form an external corner, and conceal the joint with a length of birdsmouth (corner bead) moulding.

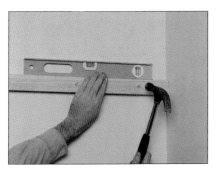

1 Tap fixing nails into each support batten at 300mm (12in) intervals. Check the batten is level and drive in the nails.

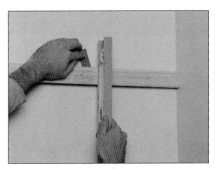

2 If the walls are out of true, insert slim packing pieces between the battens and the wall to ensure that the faces of the strips are vertical.

3 Scribe the wall outline on to the face of the first board by holding its grooved edge to the wall and running a block and pencil down it.

4 Fix the boards by interlocking their tongued-and-grooved edges and driving nails through the exposed tongue of each board into the battens.

5 When fixing subsequent boards, close up the joints by tapping the board edges with a hammer and a scrap of wood.

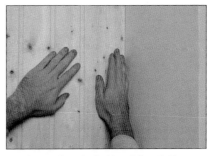

6 Saw or plane the final board down to the required width and spring the last two boards into place. Secure the last board.

BOXING-IN PIPES

Some people regard visible pipes in the home as an eyesore, but with a little time and minimal woodworking skills they can be hidden from view.

ACCESSIBILITY

Bear in mind that stopcocks, drain taps, pumps, hand-operated valves and the like will need to be readily accessible and require some form of removable box system. For this reason, the boxing around them should be assembled with screws rather than nails. If a panel needs to be regularly or quickly removed, turn buttons or magnetic catches are a good idea.

BOXING BASICS

Steel anchor plates and screws can be used to secure the sides of boxing to walls. Battens, either 50 x 25mm (2 x 1in) or 25 x 25mm (1 x 1in), can be used to fix boards at skirting (baseboard) level.

Measure the distance the pipes project from the wall. Cut the side panels from 25mm (1in) plywood or MDF (medium-density fiberboard) slightly over this measurement and to their correct length. Fix small anchor plates flush with the back edge of each panel and spaced at about 600mm (2ft) intervals.

Hold the panels against the wall and mark the screw holes. Drill them and fix the panels with plugs and screws.

Cut the front panel to size from 6mm (¼in) plywood. Drill screw holes in the panel and fix it in place.

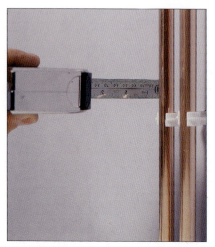

1 Measure the distance that the pipes protrude from the wall, making an allowance for any clips, brackets or fittings such as valves. Make the side panels slightly wider than this measurement.

4 Cut the front panel of the box from 6mm (¼in) plywood, using a jigsaw or circular saw. Offer it up and check the fit. If the panel does not need to be removed again, it can be nailed in place.

2 If the panels are narrow, you may be able to drive the screws through their edges – mark the positions with a pencil. If not, fix anchor plates flush with the back edges of the panels.

3 Attach the side panels, screwing them firmly into position. If screwing to a plywood panel, you may need to make pilot holes; in masonry, you need to drill and plug the holes.

5 If the panel needs to be removable, drill screw holes and secure it with 19mm (¾in) screws. Cup washers under the screw heads will protect the panel if it is likely to be removed often.

6 Trim the edges of the front panel flush with the side panels with a block plane. Then drive any nail heads below the surface and fill. Sand the entire box prior to applying a finish.

DOORS, LOCKS & WINDOWS

Among the wooden items in the home that receive a considerable amount of wear and tear are the doors. In time, you may need to replace them, either because they are damaged or to spruce up a room. Their hinges, too, can become worn and loose, or even broken. Even the doors of cabinets can suffer the same ailments, while their drawer fronts may have to be changed to match any new doors fitted. An important consideration for every householder is security – making sure that the doors and windows of your home are fitted with sturdy locks and catches that will deter a thief from breaking in. Fortunately, a wide range is available and they are not difficult to fit. A weekend's work is all that is necessary to ensure that your home is well protected.

HANGING DOORS

Installing a new door is not a difficult task, but the job does need patience, precision and organization if it is to go smoothly. A methodical step-by-step approach will pay off. The following sequence relates to hanging a new door, which may or may not need trimming on one or more sides.

TYPES OF DOOR

Many modern internal doors are hollow structures with "egg-box" centres and solid edges. They offer little flexibility for trimming to fit frames that are out of square, which is often a problem in old buildings. For this reason, as well as for aesthetic appeal, use only solid doors in older houses.

PUTTING IN A NEW DOOR

Measure the frame top to bottom and side to side, then choose a door that will fit as closely as possible. Even so, it will probably need to be cut to fit.

Joggles, or horns, may project from the ends of the door to protect it in transit. Mark these off level with the ends of the door, using a try square. Place the door on a flat surface and cut the joggles flush with the ends of the door, using a hand saw. Offer up the door to the frame, placing wedges underneath (chisels are handy) to raise it off the floor by about 12mm (½in) to allow for a carpet or other floorcovering.

Mark the door in pencil while it is wedged in place to allow for a 3mm (⅛in) clearance at the top and sides.

Place the door back on the flat surface and saw off the bulk of the waste, leaving the marked lines still visible. Plane down the edges of the door to the marked lines, working with the grain, then plane the top, working in from each side to avoid splintering the wood. Replace the door in the frame, wedging it once more to hold it. If you are satisfied with the fit, you can hang it.

Hold each hinge in position, about 150mm (6in) from the top and 225mm (9in) from the bottom of the door, with the knuckle projecting just beyond the face of the door; mark it with a knife. For a heavy door, a third hinge will be needed, positioned centrally between the other two.

Working around the outline, cut down vertically into the wood to the depth of the hinge flap with a chisel. Make a series of cuts across the width of the recess, to the same depth, and remove the waste. Place the hinge in the recess, drill small pilot holes for the screws, then screw the hinge to the door. Repeat with the other hinge.

Offer the hinge side of the door to the frame, placing wedges under it to raise it to the correct height. Press the free flap of each hinge against the frame and mark around it in pencil. Cut the recesses. Drill pilot holes and hang the door, fitting only one screw in each hinge flap. When you are satisfied with the operation of the door, insert all the screws, making sure that the heads lie flat in the countersinks of the hinges, otherwise the door will not close properly.

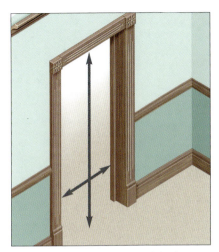

1 Measure the height and width of the door frame to assess the size of the door you require. If you cannot find the exact size needed, choose one that is slightly larger.

2 If there are protective joggles projecting from the top and bottom of the door, square them off accurately with the ends of the door, using a pencil and try or combination square.

3 Remove the joggles with a hand saw, making a clean, square cut. Saw on the waste side of the line and finish off with a plane or sanding block, working in towards the centre of the door.

4 Offer the door into the frame. Use wedges to square it up if necessary. Make sure you allow a gap of about 12mm (½in) at the bottom to accommodate the thickness of any floor covering. ▶

5 Mark the clearance between the door and frame across the top and along the sides, using a pencil and a 3mm (⅛in) washer as a guide. Join the pencil marks with a straightedge.

6 Support the door on sturdy trestles or a similar firm surface. Then saw off the bulk of the waste, using a hand saw and keeping to the waste side of the marked lines.

9 Set a marking gauge to the thickness of the hinge flap and use the gauge to mark this dimension on the face of the door, allowing the flap recess to be cut to the correct depth.

10 Chop out the waste with a sharp chisel, cutting vertically along the scribed lines first, then across the waste before scooping it out. Work carefully down to the depth of the flap.

7 Plane the edges of the door down to the marked lines. When planing the top edge, work in from both sides to prevent splintering at the ends. Offer the door into the frame to check its fit.

8 Hold each hinge on the edge of the door so that its knuckle projects just beyond the face of the door. Mark around the flap with a sharp knife or pencil.

11 Check that the flap fits snugly in the recess, flush with the door edge, making any necessary adjustments. Then make pilot holes for the screws and fix the hinge securely.

12 Mark the positions of the hinges on the door frame with a pencil. Cut the recesses and offer up the door. Fix each hinge with one screw only until you are happy with the fit.

REPLACING CABINET FRONTS

Even if they are not damaged or worn, changing the doors and drawer fronts of storage cabinets is an easy way of giving a room a new look.

NEW DRAWER FRONTS

The drawers of modern furniture are often made with false fronts that allow a basic carcass to be used in a number of different styles. To replace a front, open the drawer or, better still, remove it completely. From inside the drawer, slacken the screws holding the false front to the carcass and remove it. Place the old front over the new one, aligning it exactly, drill down through the screw holes and into the new front to make pilot holes for the fixing screws. Take care not to drill right through the new face and spoil the finish. Use a depth stop to prevent this. Finally, screw the new front to the carcass from the inside.

NEW DOORS

Replacing a chipboard (particle board) door may be necessary if the hinges have failed, which can occur with kitchen furniture after a number of years because of its heavy workload. If you replace old chipboard doors with new ones, they must be exactly the same size and be hung in the same way as the originals, since they cannot be trimmed to fit. Doors such as these are readily available, along with the chipboard hinges necessary to fit them. It is important to ensure that the hinge positions are perfectly accurate and

REPLACING A DRAWER FRONT

1 Remove the old drawer front by unscrewing it from behind.

REPLACING A DOOR

1 Remove the old hinge simply by unscrewing it from the side.

that their recesses are of the correct depth, so careful measuring and a reliable drill stand or pillar drill is essential. You will also need a special bit to cut the blind hole for the hinge in the door. Transfer the hinge positions from the old door.

2 Drill pilot holes in the new front, using the existing holes in the old one as a guide.

3 Screw the new drawer front into position from behind. Offer up the drawer and check the fit.

2 Measure accurately from the edge of the old door to the centre of the hinge hole.

3 Transfer the position to the new door to ensure that the new hinge is placed accurately.

4 Drill a new hole, preferably using a drill stand for accuracy.

5 Attach the new hinge to the new door. Then fit the door.

FITTING MORTISE DOOR LOCKS

Doors, especially those at the rear of the house, often provide an easy entrance and exit point for intruders. Good locks, properly fitted to a strong door and door frame, are the basic requirements for ensuring that house doors are secure, while additional security devices may help you feel safer at home. A mortise lock is fitted into a slot cut in the edge of a door, where it cannot easily be tampered with.

INSTALLING MORTISE LOCKS

Align the mortise lock with the centre rail of the door and use the lock body as a template for marking the top and bottom of the mortise.

Draw a line down the middle of the door edge and, using a drill bit the width of the lock body, drill a series of overlapping holes along the centre-line to the depth of the lock. Chisel out the mortise so that the lock body fits snugly. Insert the lock, mark the outline of the faceplate with a pencil and chisel out a recess so that it fits flush with the door edge.

Mark and drill the holes for the key and spindle; enlarge the keyhole with a padsaw. Assemble and check the lock works.

With the latch and bolt open, mark their positions on the frame. Measure from the outside of the door to the centre of the bolt, mark that distance on the jamb and cut mortises in this

1 Mark out the dimensions of a mortise lock on the door edge.

4 Insert the lock, then mark and chisel out the recess for the faceplate.

position. Chisel a recess for the striking plate (keeper) and check that the door closes properly before fixing.

TIP

"Measure twice and cut once."
Accuracy is vital when marking out for door locks, so take your time with this part of the job and you will experience fewer problems later.

2 Using a mortise gauge, mark a vertical line in the centre of the door between the pencil lines.

3 Drill a line of holes along the centre-line to the depth of the lock body.

5 Using the lock as a guide, mark the positions of the spindle and key holes.

6 Drill the holes, then use a padsaw to form the keyhole. Fit the covers.

7 Cut mortises for the latch and the deadbolt on the door jamb.

8 Cut out a recess for the striking plate (keeper) so that it fits flush in the door jamb.

FITTING RIM DOOR LOCKS

A rim door lock is an alternative to a mortise lock. It locks automatically as the door is closed, and the bolt cannot be forced back without a key.

INSTALLING RIM LOCKS

Mark the position of the lock on the door, using any template provided, and bore a hole with a flat bit for the key cylinder. Push the cylinder into the hole, connect the lock backplate and secure it with screws. The cylinder connecting bar will protrude through the backplate. If necessary, cut it to length using a hacksaw.

If necessary, mark and chisel out the lock recess in the door edge, then fit the lock and screw it to the door, making sure that the cylinder connecting bar has engaged in the lock.

With the door closed, mark the position of the striking plate (keeper), then chisel out the recess so that the plate fits flush with the frame. Fix the striking plate with the screws provided and check that the door closes properly.

1 Mark the position of the cylinder on the door and drill its hole.

4 If necessary, mark the length of the connecting bar to be cut off.

FITTING A RACK BOLT

A rack bolt allows you to lock a door from the inside, and is unobtrusive and secure.

Mark the position of the rack bolt in the centre of the door edge and on the inner face of the door, using a try or combination square to ensure that the two marks are level. Drill a hole of suitable size horizontally into the door edge to the depth of the body of the bolt. Push the bolt into the hole, mark the outline of the faceplate, then withdraw the bolt and chisel out a recess for the plate. Hold the bolt level with the guideline on the inside of the door, and mark and drill a hole for the key.

Fit the bolt, check that it works properly and screw the keyhole plate to the door. Close the door and wind out the bolt so that it leaves a mark. Drill a hole at this point and fit a recessed cover plate.

2 Insert the barrel of the lock cylinder into the drilled hole.

3 Fit the backplate to the door and secure it tightly with screws.

5 Fit the lock case to the connecting plate and screw together.

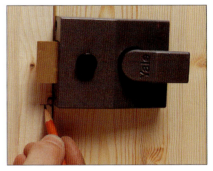

6 Mark the position of the striking plate (keeper). Chisel out its recess in the frame.

1 Use tape to mark the drilling depth and keep the bit horizontal. Push in the bolt.

2 Mark the outline of the faceplate, then withdraw the bolt to chisel out the recess.

WINDOW SECURITY

Over half of all home burglaries occur through a window, and even the smallest is vulnerable, so good locks are very important. The first line of defence is to fit good-quality handles and stays, followed by key-operated locks to all ground-floor windows, and those first-floor windows that are easily accessible. It is also essential to provide a secure means of ventilation around your home.

BASIC HARDWARE

The most common items of hardware fitted on hinged windows are a rotating cockspur handle, which is used simply to fasten the window, and a casement stay, which props it open in several different positions. On sliding sash windows, the basic hardware is a catch that locks the two sashes together when they are closed.

CHOOSING AND FITTING WINDOW LOCKS

Many window locks are surface-mounted, using screws, and are quick and easy to fit, although for some types a drilled hole for a bolt or recess chiselled for a striking plate (keeper) may be required. Mortised locks and dual screws that fit into holes drilled in the window frame take longer to install, but they are very secure.

When buying locks for windows, bear in mind the thickness of the frames. In some cases, these may be too thin to accommodate a recessed lock without seriously weakening the frame. If in any doubt, buy surface-mounted fittings.

All window locks are supplied with fixing screws, but these should often be discarded in favour of longer, more secure fixings. Some locks come with special security screws that can only be tightened, but not unscrewed. In this case, the lock should be fitted with ordinary screws first and the proper screws only added when you are happy that the lock functions correctly. In other cases, the screws are concealed by plastic plugs. For extra security, it is also a good idea to fit two locks on casement windows more than 1m (3ft) high, while all locking devices for sash windows are best used in pairs.

For secure ventilation, if the window has a stay pierced with holes, you can replace the plain peg with a casement stay lock. Attach the screw-on lock to the threaded peg with the key supplied. This will allow you to secure the window in any position.

If fitting lockable window catches and stays, do not leave keys in the locks where they might be seen by an intruder; they may also fall out as the window is opened and closed. Instead, hang them on a hook close to the window where they are readily accessible, but can't be seen from outside.

TIP

Ensure you have the right screws: a lock intended for wooden window frames requires wood screws; metal window frames will require self-tapping screws.

FITTING A WINDOW HANDLE AND STAY

1 Choose the position of the cockspur handle on the casement and make pilot holes through it with a bradawl. Then screw the handle firmly to the casement.

2 Fit the striking plate (keeper) to the frame so that it will engage with the cockspur. Drill out the frame to a depth of 20mm (¾in) through the slot in the plate.

3 Fit the casement stay by screwing its baseplate to the bottom rail of the casement, about one-third along from the hinged edge.

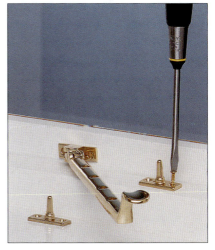

4 Open the window to find the correct position for the pegs on the frame. Attach the pegs, then fit the stay rest to the casement rail.

CASEMENT WINDOW LOCKS

Locks for wooden casement windows may be surface-mounted or set in the frame. If surface-mounted, the lockplate is attached to the fixed frame, and the body of the lock to the opening frame. With the window closed, mark the positions of the lock and plate on both frames, then screw them in place. For those with a locking bolt, you will have to cut a rebate (rabbet) or drill a hole to receive the bolt. Some surface-mounted locks are also suitable for fitting to metal casement windows. Check the instructions.

Locks that are designed to be set in the frame normally require holes to be drilled in both fixed and opening frames. Also, a hole must be drilled through the face of the frame to allow insertion of the key.

1 With the lock assembled, mark its position on the fixed and opening frames. Separate the two parts of the lock and screw the body to the opening frame.

2 Fit the cover plate and insert the screws. You may want to use longer screws than those provided to ensure a strong fixing.

3 Some makes come with small covers or plugs to hide the screws. Tap these into place when you are happy with the fit of the lock.

SASH WINDOW LOCKS

Some types of casement-window lock will also work with sash windows. An effective security device for sash windows is the sash stop, which actually allows the window to be opened slightly for ventilation. To fit the device, it is necessary to drill a hole in the upper sash to accommodate its bolt. Then a protective plate is added to the top of the lower sash. In operation, turning the key releases the spring-loaded bolt, which prevents the sashes from sliding past each other.

Another option is key-operated dual screws (shown below), which bolt both sashes together. Use a flat bit the width of the lock barrel to drill through the inner meeting rail (mullion) into the outer rail to the required depth, then tap the barrels into place with a hammer and piece of wood. Fit the longer barrel into the inner rail, the shorter into the outer rail, and screw the bolt into the barrel with the key.

FIRE SAFETY

Wherever possible, fit window locks that all use the same standard key so that any key can be used to open a window in the event of an emergency. Keep keys in accessible positions.

1 Mark the drill bit with tape to the required depth and drill through the inner meeting rail (mullion) of a sash window, into the outer rail.

2 Separate the two sections of the lock and tap the barrels of the dual screw into place in the meeting rails.

WOOD FINISHING

Practically all wooden structures need
finishing with some form of protective film
that prevents them from becoming dirty,
discoloured, or damaged by moisture or
slight knocks. Some finishes, such as wax,
allow the decorative pattern of the grain to
show through, while others, such as paint,
conceal it. Although there are many
techniques for finishing wood, a number of
basic steps are common to all of them. Carry
out preparation work well away from the
finishing area, and be prepared to move the
work back and forth several times as you
apply and rub down successive coats.
Remember that any finish on wood will
enhance defects as well as good points,
so preparation is important.

PREPARING WOOD FOR FINISHING

Many different types of wood will need filling. This can be as simple as rubbing in a grain filler, which will give a more even and less absorbent surface. It may involve using a wood filler, which can be bought to match the colour of the wood being used, to fill cracks, blemishes and knot holes. Soft interior stopping is fine for tiny cracks, and a two-part exterior-grade wood filler for making good large holes.

The tools required for finishing are simple, and most of the work can be done entirely by hand. A few scrapers, some abrasive paper in various grades, wire (steel) wool, soft cloth, a cork sanding block and some filler or stopping are the basic requirements.

Apply any filler that is necessary to knot holes and blemishes in the wood, allow to dry and remove the excess gently with a chisel. With this done, the wood can be rubbed down with abrasive paper wrapped around a cork block, working along the grain.

Wipe over the surface with a clean, damp rag to raise the grain very slightly, allow it to dry, then cut it back lightly with 400-grit abrasive paper, again working along the grain.

ESSENTIAL REQUIREMENTS

Not often mentioned is the fact that wood must be dry, regardless of the treatment applied. Another requirement is that when several applications of a finish are called for, they must be rubbed down, or "flatted", between coats.

1 Apply filler to match the colour of the wood. Scrape away any excess with a sharp chisel.

2 Sand down with abrasive paper wrapped around a cork block, working along the grain, not across it.

3 To remove dust, wipe down with a soft, damp cloth, using long strokes parallel to the grain.

STAINING AND VARNISHING WOOD

If you want to stain your wood, test the stain on a spare piece of the same wood to check the final colour and depth.

Remember that end grain will absorb a lot more of the stain and will be much darker. Stain can be applied with a soft cloth or brush. Keep a wet edge all the time to avoid a patchy finish. Apply the stain in short circular motions.

Varnishes, such as polyurethane or acrylic, which are quick drying, should be applied along the grain with a soft brush. Be sure to get into all recesses, but do not leave pools or runs. Allow to dry and flat down with 320-grit abrasive paper or a fine grade of wire (steel) wool.

Varnish is best applied in a cool environment; otherwise problems with a "ripple" finish can occur.

APPLYING STAIN

1 Use a small brush to test the colour on a spare piece of wood. Dilute the stain when treating end grain, otherwise it will be too dark.

2 If satisfied with the colour, apply the stain with a soft cloth in quick, circular motions. Don't allow the stain to "puddle".

APPLYING VARNISH

1 For large panels, use a wide brush to apply varnish with long strokes.

2 Rub down the surface using 320-grit silicon-carbide paper, varnish and repeat.

WAXING WOOD

With the wood sanded down, apply a coat of sanding sealer, lightly sanding it when dry. This provides a good base for the wax, preventing it from soaking too deeply into the wood and improving the durability of the final finish.

Apply a coat of wax to the wood with a soft cloth or a ball of very fine wire (steel) wool, using a circular motion, followed by strokes along the grain, to work it well into the wood.

Allow the wax to dry for an hour or so, then polish off with a soft cloth. Add a second, thinner, coat of wax, working in the direction of the grain only. Polish this off lightly and leave for a few hours before giving it a final vigorous polishing.

1 Apply a thin coat of clear shellac or a proprietary sanding sealer to the wood to provide a stable base for the wax. Leave this to dry, then sand lightly.

2 Apply the wax with a ball of fine wire (steel) wool, using a strong circular motion to work it into the wood. Then finish off with strokes in the direction of the grain. Allow the wax to dry.

3 Buff the wax vigorously with a polishing pad made from a soft duster. Add a second, thinner coat of wax and polish it off lightly before leaving it for a few hours. Finally, buff well.

PAINTING WOOD

Start by priming any bare areas, then apply an undercoat and finally one or two coats of gloss (oil) paint. With a standard gloss paint, begin by applying the paint vertically, and then use sideways strokes to blend it well. Work in the direction of the grain, blending in the wet edges for a uniform finish. If you are using a one-coat paint, apply the finish quite thickly in close, parallel strips and do not over-brush.

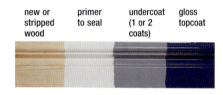

new or stripped wood	primer to seal	undercoat (1 or 2 coats)	gloss topcoat

ABOVE: The sequence for painting wood.

1 Apply a suitable primer to all areas of bare wood and allow to dry completely before over-painting. The primer will prevent the paint from soaking into the wood and leaving a patchy finish.

2 Apply one or two undercoats and lightly rub down with fine-grade abrasive paper between coats. To avoid problems, always use the same make of undercoat as topcoat.

3 Finally, apply the topcoat. When painting a panelled door, do the mouldings and panelled areas first, then move on to the cross rails, and finish with the vertical stiles.

INDEX